COOL CAREERS WITHOUT COLLEGE FOR
PEOPLE
WHO LOVE
FOOD

COOL CAREERS WITHOUT COLLEGE FOR
PEOPLE
WHO LOVE
FOOD

**KERRY
HINTON**

The Rosen Publishing Group, Inc.
New York

Published in 2004 by The Rosen Publishing Group, Inc.
29 East 21st Street, New York, NY 10010

Copyright © 2004 by The Rosen Publishing Group, Inc.

First Edition

Library of Congress Cataloging-in-Publication Data

Hinton, Kerry.
Cool careers without college for people who love food / by Kerry Hinton.— 1st ed.
    p. cm. — (Cool careers without college)
Summary: Explores the job descriptions, education and training requirements, salary, and outlook predictions for fourteen food-related careers that do not require a college education.
Includes bibliographical references and index.
ISBN 0-8239-3787-9 (library binding)
1. Cookery—Vocational guidance—Juvenile literature. [1.Cookery—Vocational guidance. 2. Vocational guidance.] I. Title. II. Series.
TX652.5 .H56 2002
641.5'023—dc21

2002006701

Manufactured in the United States of America

CONTENTS

INTRODUCTION

Food is the international language. No matter where we were born or how we were raised, we all like and need to eat. Food gives us cnergy and helps us perform well on tests and on the sports field. Food provides comfort and reminds us of home. Food is all around us. Imagine how long your day would seem without breakfast, lunch, and dinner—not to mention snacks—to break it up. And just think of the empty airtime that would be left if we removed every food-related television commercial!

Very few people view eating as a chore. In fact, most of us look forward to our next meal. We celebrate special occasions by going out to eat or making special dishes at home. Food does more than give our bodies energy; it can enrich our lives. People eat together for social reasons as well as nutritional ones. Many families use mealtimes to come together and find out how the day went for the rest of the family. In this fast-paced world, the kitchen or dining-room table may be one of the few places for everyone to gather at the same time. Eating allows for time to catch up.

If you like to cook those family meals, help people relax in a calm environment with good food, or simply want to involve food in your daily professional life, you may want to consider a career that involves the buying, preparing, or selling (and maybe eating, too) of food. Luckily, there are many jobs out there that deal with food.

The food industry is enormous, and there are far too many professions to tackle in this book. Instead, we'll cover some of the more practical jobs available. But we'll also include some fun ones you may not have considered. The majority of the jobs in this book can be attained with a high school diploma or minimal training.

A word of warning: You may want to stop reading and get something to eat before we move on. All the pictures and descriptions of food-related jobs may make you hungry!

1

FOOD SERVER

Although the job of food server seems obvious and simple, the job responsibilities are slightly more complicated. Also known as waiters and waitresses, food servers require a thorough knowledge of almost every aspect of a restaurant's operation in order to be efficient and effective at their jobs. Even though being a member of an establishment's

A waiter impresses his customers with a flaming entrée. Good waiters often enhance the experience of diners who are out for a special evening. Poor service can ruin an important occasion.

waitstaff can be tiring and demanding, it can also be a great source of income.

Job Description

At a minimum, food servers are expected to take orders, serve food, set and clear tables, and keep smiles on their faces while doing these and other tasks in a restaurant. Customer service is a huge component of gaining (and keeping) their jobs. Service with a smile really counts. Food servers should also be familiar with some of the basics of food preparation in order to help customers decide on certain menu items. Depending on the restaurant, they may be required to know more. For example, food servers may be expected to recommend the best wine to complement a meal or perform some food preparation at the customers' tables. They may even have to set a few of the more exotic dishes on fire! Servers who work at ethnic restaurants are expected to be able to interpret the menu for confused diners.

The work environment depends on where you'd be most comfortable. At coffee shops, customers are in a hurry and count on very fast service in order to get in and out in a relatively short time. On the other hand, servers who work in upscale restaurants serve customers who expect a leisurely dining experience with impeccable service. Of course, there are many restaurants that fall between these two extremes.

Many people choose waiting tables as a job because the flexible schedule gives them time to pursue other interests. The drawback is that people who wait tables rarely have a consistent weekly schedule. In addition, you should expect to have some very late or very early hours throughout your career as a food server.

If you have trouble dealing with people, this is not the job for you. No matter how many times a baby throws milk on the floor or how rude a particular customer may be, your job depends on the three C's: being cool, calm, and collected.

A Day in the Life of a Waiter or Waitress

Let's imagine you've been hired as a member of the waitstaff at your local bistro. You have the 5 PM to 11 PM shift. What do you do?

4:30 PM

A pre-shift employee meal is served, usually at a discount, but you have to arrive before your shift to take advantage of it.

5:15 PM

Be in your full serving uniform. Head to the staff meeting, where you'll learn the evening's specials, your table section assignment, and the "86 list" (what the restaurant is out of).

5:30 PM

Start your premial (pronounced PREE-mee-ul) work, which is just fancy talk for making sure all of the tables in your section are set and have condiment dispensers that are full and clean.

6:00 PM

Wait on your first table of the evening.

10:00 PM

Kitchen closes. Start your sidework (post-shift) work, which is the reverse of your premial work. Clean coffee machines and tables. Be considerate and leave a clean section for the next day's first shift.

10:30 PM

Cash out—that is, collect your money and tips.

11:00 PM

Head home.

A final word: Waiting tables is a very physical job. You should be in fairly good shape, since you'll constantly be on your feet and may have to carry heavy trays of food.

Education and Training

Most food servers learn how to do their jobs as they go. Many restaurants have a brief orientation to help servers become comfortable with the specifics of a particular restaurant, but they expect new employees to learn the ropes quickly.

It would be unrealistic to walk into an upscale restaurant and expect a job immediately. These establishments require a good deal of waiting experience. Waiters and waitresses at the fanciest restaurants need to be able to perform the basics

Waiters and waitresses often have to balance heavy trays of food as they go through busy kitchens and the narrow aisles of the dining areas.

perfectly before they can be expected to perform more complicated tasks. The best advice is to start early and take a part-time job as a waiter or waitress while you are in school. This experience will give you a great advantage later on if you are serious about pursuing this line of work.

Salary

The base salary of a food server is very low. Some restaurants actually pay below the hourly minimum wage level.

Food servers often do more than serve food to customers, especially in diners where employees often perform double duty. In this photo, a short-order cook cleans the counter on which he will serve the food he prepares.

In exchange, they allow the staff to keep the tips that diners give their servers. Restaurants that have a wealthier clientele and more expensive menus may pay a higher hourly rate. In 2000, the average hourly wage for waiters and waitresses was $6.42 an hour, but some made as much as $10.15 an hour.

While the majority of jobs waiting tables do not provide medical or retirement benefits, they may offer different perks, such as free or discounted meals.

Outlook

According to the most recent edition of the *Job Outlook Handbook*, the outlook for waiters and waitresses is good. Because of the high turnover rate within the field, many businesses are often on the lookout for new employees.

FOR MORE INFORMATION

ORGANIZATIONS

National Restaurant Association Education Foundation
175 West Jackson Boulevard, Suite 1500
Chicago, IL 60604-2702
(800) 765-2122
Web site: http://www.nraef.org
This organization supports the National Restaurant Association in offering professional development, education, and licensing and certification in restaurant-related jobs.

WEB SITES

On the Rail
http://www.ontherail.com
A resource for restaurant and food service workers, with job listings from deli help to chefs.

Waiter Digest
http://www.schonwalder.org
A site with information on food and wine, as well as some waiter/waitress humor.

BOOKS

Brown, Bob. *The Little Brown Book of Restaurant Success*. Tampa, FL: Acheiveglobal, 1994.
A valuable guide for hopeful waiters and waitresses, restaurant managers, and just about anyone who performs some function in a restaurant.

Casado, Matt A. *Food and Beverage Service Manual.* New York: John Wiley and Sons, 1994.
This is a great reference guide for anyone who needs a handy guide to keep the big picture of serving patrons in focus. Includes many informative drawings and diagrams.

Dahmer, Sondra J. *The Waiter and Waitress Training Manual*. New York: John Wiley and Sons, 1995.
Dahmer lays out all the facts on waiting tables for both aspiring waiters and waitresses and the people who train them. This comprehensive volume covers every aspect of table service from proper uniform hints to serving food to wine suggestions for various meals.

Devoss, Lishka. *How to Be a Professional Waiter (Or Waitress): Everything You Need to Know to Get the Right Job, Make Good Money, and Stay Sane*. New York: St. Martin's Press, 1995.
A comprehensive guide with no-nonsense, practical advice on how to make a living as a waiter or a waitress.

Ginsburg, Debra. *Waiting: The True Confessions of a Waitress.* New York: HarperCollins, 2000.
The real scoop on what it's like to be a waitress from someone who spent twenty years in this career.

Kirkham, Mike, Bill Crawford, and Peggy Weiss. *The Waiting Game: The Ultimate Guide to Waiting Tables*. Austin, TX: Twenty Per Cent LLC, 2000. As the authors of this book say, "Before you can win you have to know how to play the game," and they do a good job of giving readers as much information as possible in an entertaining and attention-holding format. This book is even endorsed by First Lady Laura Bush.

Lewis, Leslie N. *Waiter, There's a Fly in My Soup: How to Make Megabucks Waiting Tables.* New York: Bookmark Publishing Company, 1998. Good advice on how to maximize tips from customers through friendly and efficient service.

2

RESTAURANT MANAGER

A good restaurant manager needs to be in control and aware of almost everything that occurs in his or her workplace. If you don't mind long hours and a lot of responsibility, and would like to work with people who want to serve a good meal and provide good service, you may want to consider this career.

Restaurant managers are often heavily involved in setting menus. Communicating with customers and the waitstaff helps them decide what will sell.

Job Description

Managing a restaurant requires organization, a solid understanding of basic business principles, and a good idea of how the food service industry operates. For better or worse, managing a restaurant will separate you from the rest of the employees. You may find yourself having to fire people who can't obey basic rules like showing up on time, or worse, employees who are stealing from the business. Restaurant managers have to ensure that everything is going smoothly between the floor staff and the kitchen staff.

Restaurant managers also need to know a lot about food. A chef may create the dishes a restaurant serves, but many restaurant managers approve the ingredients and help decide what source will supply them. The manager may also work with chefs and cooks to come up with creative ideas (such as new menu items and special promotions) and make sure the business adheres to a previously determined food budget.

Be prepared to work quite a few hours if you choose to be a restaurant manager. While it is a fun and interesting job, you may be called upon to handle unplanned crises that arise. If the ice machine breaks or if a pipe in the men's rest room bursts, you can't go home, even if your shift is over.

"Supervise" is another word for "manage," and you will often be called upon to do just that. If work is not accomplished, you are ultimately to blame. Giving people tasks to perform is only the beginning. It takes exceptional personal skills to know how to see those tasks through. Good management often means encouraging a team environment to create a general good vibe. If employees feel that their manager is behind them, they will probably do better and more productive work.

Education and Training

Many managers start in entry-level positions—beginning their careers as cooks, hosts, bartenders, or food servers—and work their way up to management. Previous restaurant

A restaurant manager and a fish vendor negotiate prices at a fish market. Some restaurant managers serve as their establishments' food buyers.

experience is important because it gives managers a better understanding of their employees and the difficulties of their individual jobs. The average restaurant manager spends three or four years in the trenches, gaining all the knowledge he or she needs to run a restaurant.

Salary

Restaurant managers are normally paid a salary rather than an hourly wage. The salary is dependent on the area in which they work, because factors such as the cost of living directly affect salary. As of 2002, the average restaurant manager's annual salary is approximately $40,000, but some earn more than $47,000.

Outlook

The high turnover in the food service industry provides management opportunities to people who decide to stick it out for a while. If you think this career sounds interesting, give it a try, but remember to be patient. The longer you work for a manager, the better you will perform once you are called on to fill his or her shoes.

Profile

Eleven Questions with Cameron Shosh

Manager, Mile Square Restaurant, Hoboken, New Jersey

HOW LONG HAVE YOU BEEN IN THE RESTAURANT BUSINESS?

Seven years.

HOW MANY PEOPLE WORK FOR YOU?

I manage a staff of fifty people.

WHAT ARE YOUR HOURS LIKE? DO YOU HAVE A SET SCHEDULE?

A lot of hours, but I do have a set schedule. I work five days a week from 10 AM to 5 PM, and I have one long weekend day—10:30 AM to midnight.

WHAT CAN YOU EXPECT IN YOUR FIRST TWO HOURS OF WORK?

I need to make sure that supplies I've ordered have arrived, talk with the chef about daily specials, check reservations for the day, and check our 86 list, which is an inventory of items we may be out of.

WHAT OTHER JOBS HAVE YOU HAD IN RESTAURANTS?

I've been a grill cook, a waiter, a bartender, and an expediter.

WHOM DO YOU REPORT TO?

I report to the restaurant's owner. I talk to him at least once a week at our staff meetings.

DO YOU CONTRIBUTE TO THE RESTAURANT'S MENU?

Yes. I have the opportunity to look at item sales and make recommendations.

DOES TECHNOLOGY PLAY A BIG PART IN YOUR JOB?

We have a computer-based ordering system that the waiters and waitresses use to input orders, which are transmitted to the bar and kitchen. The computer also helps me control my inventory and budget.

IS IT HARD TO DISCIPLINE EMPLOYEES?

There's a high turnover in restaurants and it's hard to find people who can take discipline or criticism without wanting to leave. I try to find a happy medium so both the employees and I are happy.

DO YOU HAVE TO DEAL WITH RUDE CUSTOMERS?

All the time!

DO YOU LIKE YOUR JOB?

Yes. I like dealing with people on a daily basis. And even though the hours are tough, I love the responsibility I have.

FOR MORE INFORMATION

ORGANIZATIONS

National Restaurant Association
1200 17th Street NW
Washington, DC 20036
(202) 331-5900
Web site: http://www.restaurant.org
According to its Web site, the National Restaurant Association's mission is to represent, educate, and promote a rapidly growing industry that is composed of 858,000 restaurant and food service outlets employing 11.3 million people.

Society for Foodservice Management
304 West Liberty Street
Suite 201
Louisville, KY 40202
(502) 583-3783
Web site: http://www.sfm-online.org
A national association serving executives in the food service industry, the society helps its members achieve career and business objectives.

WEB SITES

Foodshow.com
http://www.foodshow.com
A good resource for trade associations related to food service.

BOOKS

Axler, Bruce H., and Carol Litrides, contributor. *Food and Beverage Service*. New York: John Wiley and Sons, 1990.
A reference guide that covers every aspect of food and beverage service.

Brown, Douglas Robert. *The Restaurant Manager's Handbook: How to Set Up, Operate and Manage a Financially Successful Food Service Operation*. Ocala, FL: Atlantic Publishing Company, 1989.
A detailed and helpful guide for anyone interested in any level of the restaurant business. This is a great resource for business owners and managers alike.

Marvin, Bill. *Guest-Based Marketing: How to Increase Restaurant Sales Without Breaking Your Budget*. New York: John Wiley and Sons, 1997.
An economically minded book that discusses inexpensive ways to drum up more business without having to spend tremendous amounts of money.

Marvin, Bill. *Restaurant Basics: Why Guests Don't Come Back...and What You Can Do About It.* New York: John Wiley and Sons, 1991. A guide to keeping customers satisfied and in your restaurant.

Steadman, Dave. *Restaurant Biz Is Showbiz! Why Marketing Is the Key to Your Success.* Greenlawn, NY: Spirited Living Publishing, 1991. An interesting book that gives advice on how to increase restaurant profits while keeping a restaurant fun, friendly, and comfortable.

PERIODICALS

Nation's Restaurant News (NRN).
425 Park Avenue, 6th Floor
New York, NY 10022
Web site: http://www.nrn.com
NRN's print and online components cover current industry news, franchise information, and upcoming tradeshow schedules.

Restaurant & Institutions
Cahners Business Information
8878 South Barrons Boulevard
Highlands Ranch, CO 80129-2345
Web site: http://www.rimag.com
A print magazine that covers restaurant and staff issues. Also includes innovative recipes and menu selections along with a helpful classifieds listing for job seekers.

Restaurant Report Magazine
811 North Fairway Road
North Hills, PA 19038
Web site: http://www.restaurantreport.com
A print and online magazine with articles covering the most current debates among restaurateurs, as well as happenings in restaurants worldwide.

SLAMMED
38 Jarvis Avenue
Hingham, MA 02043
Web site: http://www.slammedmagazine.com
A print magazine based in New England with a very youthful and fun approach to the restaurant industry.

COOK

For the record, there is a difference between a chef and a cook. We'll discuss chefs and their responsibilities a little later. Cooks can be found in diners, chain restaurants, burger joints, and fast-food restaurants. They can also be found in large institutions, such as schools, hospitals, camps, and companies.

Short-order cooks make simple, easy-to-prepare meals in places that offer limited fare but provide quick service, such as diners and coffee shops.

Job Description

The major difference between cooks and chefs is that cooks work from a previously created menu and usually have very little if any input into what goes on a menu. Many cooks prepare food on an as-needed basis, meaning that they fill orders as they are made by customers. A short-order cook at a hamburger stand cooks each hamburger as it is ordered, rather than grilling up a big batch in the morning and selling them throughout the day. Stews, soups, and sauces that can be kept at a steady temperature and remain fresh over longer periods of time are sometimes made in bulk at the start of a day or shift and dispensed as they are requested.

In addition to cooking the food that is served, cooks also have to be very clean and extremely conscious of maintaining a clean workspace. It is incredibly easy for people to become ill if food is not prepared in the cleanest conditions. Certain foods cannot be served with the utensil they were prepared with. This is serious business, and it takes a dedicated cook to remember and apply guidelines and laws regarding health and sanitation regulations.

A counterpart to the short-order cook is the institutional cook. The job is similar to that of a short-order cook, but the major difference is volume. What qualifies as an institution? Hospitals, high school cafeterias, and lunchrooms in office buildings all qualify. All of these places have dozens, maybe even hundreds of people who eat at roughly the same time

A kitchen assistant lines up cheeseburgers at a high school cafeteria in Cedar Falls, Iowa, that caters to more than 1,500 students each day.

once or twice a day. Imagine how much soup has to be prepared for a thousand hungry high school students! Most institutional cooks have assistants or work in teams in order to complete their tasks quickly. The ingredients alone for a high school lunch period (think fifty-pound bags of rice) may be too heavy for one cook to lift.

Education and Training

Most cooks need to have a high school diploma in order to be hired. Apprenticeships are very important to the food industry in general, and cooking is no exception. Even if you are a whiz

Typically, short-order cooks work on several orders at a time, especially during peak hours when the orders come in at a furious pace. The cook must work quickly, yet prepare meals the customers find satisfying.

with macaroni and cheese at home, it is unlikely that you will be able to walk into your first job and nab the head cook position. Start out after school or on weekends on a part-time basis if you are really interested. By the time you finish high school, you will have a year or two under your belt, and this will help you immensely if you want to move up at your job or seek employment elsewhere.

Salary

Short-order cooks can make between $21,000 and $31,000 per year. The location of a restaurant or the number of

Diner Lingo

Part of the fun of going to a diner or luncheonette is listening to the waiters or waitresses yelling out their orders. Adam and Eve on a raft? Groundhog? What are they talking about?

Trying to decipher the shorthand slang between diner cooks and servers is sometimes more enjoyable than the food. Some terms like short stack and BLT, have become part of our vocabulary. But others may have you scratching your head. Here are some of the more interesting substitutions:

CODE	WHAT IT MEANS
Adam's ale	water
cow juice	milk
birdseed	cereal
bowl of red	bowl of chili
bowwow	hot dog
burn the British	toast an English muffin
breath	onion
deadeye	poached egg
dog biscuit	cracker
draw one	get some coffee

fifty-five	glass of root beer
houseboat	banana split
lumber	toothpick
java	coffee
on the hoof	meat cooked rare
no cow	without milk
wreck 'em	scramble some eggs

patrons may directly affect the salary. The amount of business a restaurant does can often be reflected in the money its employees earn.

Institutional cooks make slightly less than short-order cooks, but more experienced cooks can make over $30,000. Also, a benefits package is often part of the deal.

Outlook

Fifty-four billion meals are eaten in school cafeterias and work lunchrooms every year. That's billions of hamburgers and slices of pizza. There is usually work to be found for cooks because many people move in and out of the industry. If business slows in one area, a cook may have to move to where the work is.

FOR MORE INFORMATION

WEB SITES

Canadian Federation of Chefs and Cooks (CFCC)
http://www.cfcc.ca
An organization of professional chefs and cooks in Canada.

Diner Soft
http://www.dinersoft.com
A site for people who work in restaurants or who just like going to them.

Food Service Central
http://www.foodservicecentral.com
A resource for everyone in the food service industry.

Hospitality Jobs Online
http://www.hotel-jobs.com
A service with jobs in the business of hospitality, which includes hotels and cooking.

Job Bank USA
http://jobbankusa.com
An in-depth job search engine, listing many employment opportunities in the food services industry.

On the Rail
http://www.ontherail.com
A Web site dealing with issues that are important to food service workers.

BOOKS

Boyle, Tish, and Clark Irey, photographer. *Diner Desserts.* San Francisco: Chronicle Books, 2000.
A cookbook for anyone who has a sweet tooth or who wants to make something sweet. This book covers it all—from ice-cream sodas to apple pie to cheesecake.

Gutman, Richard J. *American Diner.* New York: Harper Perennial, 1993.
Mr. Gutman's book offers a great history of one of the largest employers of short-order cooks in the world—diners. He discusses the history of diners and their importance as a part of North American culture. Filled with fun pictures and odd fun-facts, this book is a great read.

Kleiman, Evan. *Pizzeria: The Best of Casual Pizza Oven Cooking* (Casual Cuisines of the World). Menlo Park, CA: Sunset Publishing Company, 1997.
Every short-order cook should have a pizza recipe or two in his or her bag of tricks, and this book is a great place for some traditional and off-the-wall recipes direct from the pizza kitchens of Italy.

Lloyd, Tim, and James Novak. *Blue Plate Diner Cookbook.* Madison, WI: Prairie Oak Press, 1999.
A cookbook filled with some of the best and most original dishes served by the people at the Blue Plate Diner in Madison, Wisconsin.

Maddocks, Rick. *Sputnik Diner.* New York: Knopf, 2002.
The story of a diner in Ontario, Canada, and the lives of the memorable people who work there and those who pass through.

McKeon, Elizabeth, and Linda Everett. *Blue Plate Special: The American Diner Cookbook.* Nashville, TN: Cumberland House, 1996.
A great collection of diner and diner-style recipes to try out, including one for homemade ketchup!

Pawlcyn, Cindy. *Fog City Diner Cookbook.* Berkeley, CA: Ten Speed Press, 1993.
Another batch of recipes from an honest-to-goodness diner, San Francisco's Fog City Diner.

Sample, Tim, and Stephen King. *Saturday Night at Moody's Diner: Even More Stories*. Camden, ME: Down East Books, 1996.
A collection of stories that center around Moody's, a diner in Maine.

Worthington, Diane Rossen, and Allan Rosenberg. *Diner: The Best of Casual American Cooking* (Casual Cuisines of the World). Menlo Park, CA: Sunset Publishing Company, 1995.
Fifty recipes for "classic American dishes" that simulate the ultimate diner experience in the comfort of one's own home.

CHEF

Chefs are artists—their canvas is a plate and they paint with food. They spend countless hours devising, concocting, and conjuring amazing dishes. These meals are the result of well-organized, creative, and efficient minds.

Job Description

There are different types of chefs, all of whom have the common goal of

A group of chefs working in a restaurant's kitchen. If you have a multicourse meal at a restaurant, it is likely that several chefs will be involved in its preparation.

keeping a restaurant kitchen running smoothly. Everyone on a chef's team, or line, needs to possess a great sense of smell and taste.

Prep cooks are not involved with the actual cooking of food. They prepare the ingredients of a particular meal on a planned menu. This can range from peeling potatoes or shrimp to mincing garlic to chopping fresh herbs. Most prep cooks hope to become chefs, and this position is a great stepping stone because it allows them to develop

important skills and techniques, and get accustomed to a professional kitchen.

Garde-mangers (pronounced "mahn-jays") are in charge of all cold food that comes off the cooking line. This involves all kinds of dishes, including salads, hors d'oeuvres, and various parts of buffets. Some garde-mangers may need to be proficient at creating ice sculptures for a food display.

Sauciers are very specialized members of a kitchen line. Their main job is to create sauces. In traditional kitchens, sauciers are almost like chemists, using five basic sauces in various combinations to concoct hundreds of different new sauces. Every saucier has his or her own special ingredients and measurements, which make every creation of every saucier a different experience.

Pastry chefs are as specialized as sauciers, but their area of expertise lies in the making of delicious desserts. Pastry chefs are slightly different from bakers because they usually have chef's training and have to know how to create a wider variety of desserts. Most pastry chefs gain experience from cooking meals before they choose to focus on desserts.

Sous (pronounced SOO) chefs are the right-hand men and women who support the executive chef. Sous chefs may be responsible for the actual cooking of a meal while the head chef supervises other tasks going on in a kitchen. Some sous chefs perform in place of the executive chef if he or she

is away, and some exist in more of an apprentice role, watching and learning on their way to becoming an executive chef.

The executive chef, or head chef, is the end of the line as far as responsibility goes. The head chef needs to be in control and aware of everything that goes in and out of his or her kitchen. Executive chefs are in the position to receive both blame and praise, but the positive aspects of the job are immensely satisfying and rewarding.

Executive chefs often oversee the purchase of the food to be cooked and the budget used to buy it. Depending on the restaurant, executive chefs may also interview and train employees, obtain cooking equipment, and plan banquets.

Education and Training

The quickest way to get on track as a chef is to go to culinary school. There are many schools in the United States and Canada that offer culinary programs. Many chefs learn the old-fashioned way, however, and work their way up through the ranks by watching and learning from the more experienced chefs in the kitchen. If you have an aptitude for cooking and are not going to attend a cooking school, try

A chef serves a couple from an elaborate buffet. Chefs take great pride in the way their meals are presented.

your hand working as a cook or a member of a line in a restaurant. Another option is to take occasional classes while you work in a restaurant to improve your skills.

Salary

Salaries for chefs vary. A factor in this is restaurant size and location. A chef who cooks for 100 customers in a busy city has the opportunity to make a larger income than one who works in a less populated area. Sous chefs with experience average about $36,000 a year, and members of the line below them can expect to make a few thousand dollars less per year. Pastry chefs can make up to $60,000 a year, due to the fact that they have spent more time in the business. The average executive chef is paid $52,000 a year, but he or she can make $200,000 a year, according to a survey conducted by the National Restaurant Association.

Outlook

Statistics from the Department of Labor indicate that employment opportunities for chefs will continue to increase through the year 2005. More than 3.4 million chefs and kitchen workers were employed in the last five years. There is a substantial amount of turnover in the food industry, so dedicated and persistent people who stay involved

A student attends to a wedding cake she is displaying at a culinary arts festival. Young people who aspire to become chefs should seriously consider attending a culinary school.

long enough can rise to the top with some smarts and a good book of recipes. Besides working in a traditional restaurant, chefs have the added options of heading up cooking lines in hospitals, colleges, and casinos. Some chefs also decide to take their skills to the classroom and pass these skills on to a whole new generation of hopeful culinary whiz kids.

FOR MORE INFORMATION

ORGANIZATIONS

American Culinary Federation

10 San Bartola Drive
St. Augustine, FL 32086
(800) 624-9458
Web site: http://www.acfchefs.org
A national chefs organization for the United States. Provides certification and education information and more.

SCHOOLS

Culinary Institute of America

1946 Campus Drive
Hyde Park, NY 12538
(845) 452-9600
Web site: http://www.ciachef.edu
One of the best-known schools solely dedicated to cooking in the United States.

Whistler Cooking School

119-4295 Blackcomb Way
Whistler, BC V0N 1B4
Canada
(604) 935-1848
Web site: http://www.whistlercookingschool.com
A Canadian school that offers full- and part-time classes for hopeful chefs.

WEB SITES

Chef Desk—Resources for Chefs
http://www.chefdesk.com
Nice site by Chef Francis Lynch, featuring online conversion calculators for food measurements and more.

Cooking & Culinary Arts Schools
http://www.cooking-culinary-arts-schools.com
This is a great Web site that has a directory of dozens of cooking and culinary schools.

Shaw Guides
http://cookforfun.shawguides.com
An online guide to cooking schools, with plenty of valuable information.

BOOKS

Bittman, Mark. *How to Cook Everything: Simple Recipes for Great Food*. New York: Macmillan, 1998.
A food writer for the *New York Times*, Bittman offers recipes and variations on those recipes for almost anything you could imagine. This book is a must for the beginning chef.

Child, Julia, Louisette Bertholle, and Simone Beck. *Mastering the Art of French Cooking, Volume One*. New York: Knopf, 2001.
Julia Child is known throughout the world as an expert on anything kitchen related, and in this book she discusses the basics and finer points of cooking French cuisine.

Claiborne, Craig, and Pierre Franey. *The New New York Times Cookbook*. New York: Random House, 1995.
A comprehensive cookbook used by chefs, containing over 1,000 recipes, including ethnic and regional cuisine.

Diamond, Marilyn. *The American Vegetarian Cookbook from the Fit for Life Kitchen*. New York: Warner Books, 1990.
An informative cookbook with a special focus on vegetarian cooking and nutritious recipes for use at home.

Jamison, Cheryl Alters, and Bill Jamison. *American Home Cooking: Over 300 Spirited Recipes Celebrating Our Rich Tradition of Home Cooking.* New York: Broadway Books, 1999.
A cookbook dedicated to the art of home cooking.

Rombauer, Irma S., et al. *The New Joy of Cooking.* New York: Scribner, 1997.
One of the best-known cookbooks ever published, it began as a collection of recipes from friends and relatives. This new edition contains the original recipes plus new recipes that involve grains and soybeans for alternative diets.

PERIODICALS

Cook's Illustrated
Boston Common Press
17 Station Street
Brookline, MA 02445
A print and online magazine for the at-home cook. A great tool for chefs who strive for a personal touch.

Gourmet
Condé Nast Publications
4 Times Square
New York, NY 10036
Web site: http://www.condenet.com/mags/gmet
A print and online magazine that combines travel and a love of food to examine great food across the globe.

Vegetarian Times
International Subscriptions Inc.
1 Meadowlands Plaza, 9th Floor
East Rutherford, NJ 07073
Web site: http://www.vegetariantimes.com
A print and online magazine concerned with vegetarian cuisine. The magazine includes important items such as food substitutions for vegetarians, natural remedies, nutritional information, and a glossary for new vegetarians.

PERSONAL CHEF

Personal chefs are cooks-for-hire who do not work in a traditional restaurant setting. Instead, they usually bring food to their clients. Some personal chefs have experience cooking in restaurants and have decided to put a slightly different twist on their profession. Some have cooked for their own families for years and are pursuing a new line of work.

Many people become personal chefs because they want to have a greater say in what they cook rather than being confined to a restaurant's menu, which is likely to be set for months at a time.

Sometimes personal chefs cook solely for one person or family, but usually they have multiple clients to whom they bring food.

Job Description

Personal chefs have the opportunity to enjoy more creative freedom at an earlier stage in their cooking careers. It takes years of work to become the head chef at many restaurants. Until then, many chefs spend a good deal of time assisting head chefs, who ultimately decide which dishes will be served. Starting your own business puts you in charge, and with the added responsibility that involves, you can be rewarded with the chance to develop your own unique culinary creations.

The food personal chefs prepare varies widely. Some prepare familiar or "comfort" foods like steak or lasagna, while some have to cook foods according to special dietary needs for people with medical concerns. For example, if a child is allergic to milk, a personal chef needs to adjust his or her menu. Some personal chefs may work for clients who are accustomed to more complicated menu selections.

Personal chefs usually do more than cook. They most likely have a budget they must adhere to when buying food. Knowing where to get the best and freshest ingredients is also a plus. Organizational skills are also very important in this profession. The majority of personal chefs do not decide to "wing it" when they arrive at their clients' houses—they come prepared with preplanned menus. Some personal chefs may never see the families they cook for and may need to freeze or refrigerate their creations with preparation instructions.

In addition to having fewer clients at a time, most personal chefs get the chance to see their clients frequently and develop a more personal relationship with the people who eat and

Some personal chefs prepare meals in their own kitchens and then deliver them to their clients.

enjoy their food. Some personal chefs may even live in the house of the family whose food they prepare. In these cases, they are referred to as "private chefs." The chance to have great working relationships and possibly friendships with an employer is a great bonus in this line of work.

Education and Training

To be a personal chef, you must be experienced in the art of cooking and have a thorough knowledge of food preparation, food storage, and nutrition. Personal chefs also need to be flexible and friendly. People skills aren't just a plus in this job—they're a necessity. Restaurants have kitchen doors to separate the staff from the clientele, and rarely do the two meet. That line doesn't really exist for personal chefs.

You can become a personal chef without training. Personal chef Sharon Worster, who was a nurse in Texas for seventeen years, loved to cook for her family. Once she spotted an article on cooking for smaller groups as a personal chef, she was hooked. Today, she owns her own personal chef service in Texas.

Some personal chefs do complete courses of study at professional cooking schools, which gives them formal training and an immediate foundation for starting a business, but it is not required. One option is to combine the two approaches and start your career as a personal chef learning in the workplace and gather as much experience as you can before setting out to be an entrepreneur.

Once you decide you're ready to strike out on your own as a personal chef, it may be a good idea to join a personal chef's association to help you find work in your field, and also to meet people who have done the job for some time. Associations like these offer certification programs. The field is very competitive now, and some qualification will assist you if a potential client chooses to interview you.

Salary

Many personal chefs are paid by the hour. In New York City, personal chefs can make between $25 and $45 per hour. Given that many personal chefs serve at least a few clients, a dedicated and efficient one could make up to $300 a day.

Outlook

The number of families with two working parents is growing, and so is the need for personal chefs. Hiring a personal chef enables busy families to come home and enjoy a well-prepared meal. In 2000, *Entrepreneur* magazine stated that the personal chef business is one of the twelve fastest growing businesses in the United States. The American Personal Chef Institute Association has 2,000 current members, with 100 new chefs joining the ranks each week!

FOR MORE INFORMATION

ORGANIZATIONS
American Personal Chef Association
4572 Delaware Street
San Diego, CA 92116
(800) 644-8389

Web site: http://www.personalchef.com
Professional organization for personal chefs in the United States.

Canadian Personal Chef Association

100 Broadview Avenue, Suite 302
Toronto, ON M4M 3H3
Canada
(800) 995-2138
Web site: http://www.canadianpersonalchef.com
Professional association for personal chefs in Canada.

United States Personal Chef Association (USPCA)

481 Rio Rancho Boulevard NE
Rio Rancho, NM 87124
(800) 995-2138
Web site: http://www.uspca.com
An organization devoted to the personal chef.

WEB SITES

CookingSchools.com

http://www.cookingschools.com
Billed as the cooking and culinary school directory, this Web site has a wealth of information and includes a great interview with well-known personal chef Sharon Worster.

BOOKS

Berry, Mary, and Marlena Spieler. *Classic Home Cooking*. New York: DK Publishing, 1995.
An easy-to-read cookbook for beginners and professionals, with full-color pictures for each recipe discussed. Also includes advice on microwaving, freezing and reheating, and presentation ideas.

Diamond, Marilyn. *The American Vegetarian Cookbook from the Fit for Life Kitchen*. New York: Warner Books, 1990.
An informative cookbook with a special focus on vegetarian cooking and nutritious recipes for at-home use.

Jamison, Cheryl Alters, and Bill Jamison. *American Home Cooking: Over 300 Spirited Recipes Celebrating Our Rich Tradition of Home Cooking.* New York: Broadway Books, 1999.
A cookbook dedicated to the art of home cooking.

Morgan, Jorj. *At Home in the Kitchen: The Art of Preparing the Foods You Love to Eat.* Nashville, TN: Cumberland House, 2001.
A cookbook with inventive twists on well-known, traditional, home-cooked recipes for the entire family.

Rombauer, Irma S., et al. *The New Joy of Cooking.* New York: Scribner, 1997.
One of the best-known cookbooks ever published, which began as a collection of recipes from friends and relatives. This new edition contains the original recipes plus new recipes that involve grains and soybeans for alternative diets.

PERIODICALS
Bon Appétit
Condé Nast Publications
4 Times Square
New York, NY 10036
Web site: http://eat.epicurious.com/bonappetit
Print and online magazine dedicated to good food and its enjoyment. Includes articles on food, wine, and cook's tools. The online portion, Epicurious, features the "world's greatest recipe collection."

Fine Cooking
The Taunton Press
63 South Main Street
P.O. Box 5506
Newtown, CT 06470-5506
Web site: http://taunton.com/finecooking
A print and online magazine for chefs and people who like to cook at home. The Web site has a special link to the Cooks Talk Forum, a newsgroup for professional chefs, amateur chefs, and everyone in between.

Gourmet Connection
CAPCO Marketing, Inc.
P.O. Box 842
Baldwinsville, NY 13027
Web site: http://gourmetconnection.com/ezine
A print and online magazine that covers gourmet cooking and in-depth discussion of health issues related to food and various food ingredients.

BAKER

Chocolate cake. Sugar cookies. Dutch apple pie. Cinnamon rolls. Banana nut bread. These could be the first five items on your daily "to-do" list if you decide to become a baker. Bakers produce some of the sweetest and most mouth-watering treats, and get a paycheck for it. Nice work if you can get it! And if you *do* want to get this type of work, read on!

To build and retain a loyal customer base, it is important that bakers make sure their products are consistent in taste, appearance, and overall quality. Bakers must take great care when measuring, mixing, and baking.

Job Description

Bakers work in bakeries or bakeshops and spend their days making delicious baked goods for customers to enjoy. A baker does much more than open a box of cake mix and go to work. The key phrase for most bakers is "from scratch." This means that good bakers can take flour, eggs, butter, and milk, and transform them into birthday cakes or strudel.

Bakers need a good eye for detail because they spend much of their time following recipes and weighing, measuring, and mixing ingredients. Incorrect measurements don't result in dishes that taste good in the baking world, so bakers need to be precise in their calculations. The sign of a great baker is one who can improvise ingredients or add his or her own special touch to a common recipe. However, many bakeries request that bakers follow only preselected recipes.

Safety is a big concern for any baker. The temperatures of baking ovens are extremely hot, and the simple process of placing a baking tray in an oven can become dangerous if safety precautions are not followed. The heat from the ovens also makes bakery kitchens extremely warm, which can be a difficult environment to work in.

Bakeries usually order ingredients in large quantities to keep a sufficient amount on hand at all times. A bakery without flour might as well not be open for business. Large bags of flour or cornmeal are heavy. Combined with the stress of standing on one's feet for a ten- to twelve-hour day, bakers run the risk of straining their backs from lifting and stooping often.

Bakers often work long hours and have to be up very early. This is not a career for late sleepers. Many bakeries that open to the public at 8 AM have had their ovens working for a few hours before that, concocting the freshest pastries and rolls for customers who demand quality. The average baker at a local bakery works at least a forty-hour workweek.

Some bakeries may employ more than one baker; this is usually the case for larger bakeries. There are also some experienced bakers who may eventually perform only one

Baking is hard work. In addition to spending long hours in sweltering heat, bakers do a lot of heavy lifting.

job. Your local bakery will most likely have a baker or two and possibly an assistant. Bakers can also write for food magazines, as well as instruct classes in vocational and culinary schools. A few may even have the opportunity to appear on local or national cooking shows on television.

Education and Training

Since a college degree is not needed to become a baker, apprenticing is the best way to start your career in baking. An apprentice is a person who works under the supervision of a

Because pastries are expected to be pleasing to the eye as well as the palate, bakers spend a lot of time decorating their products.

professional while he or she learns the basics of a job. Bakers' apprentices get a chance to earn a wage while learning the craft from an experienced baker. Apprenticeships are not readily available, so get a head start on the competition by starting as soon as possible. See if the local bakery or supermarket baked-goods section needs part-time help. Chances are you won't be decorating cakes when you start—most bakery helpers spend their hours on the job cleaning pots, rolling pins, and mixing bowls.

If you attend a vocational high school, baking may be offered as a course or included in the coursework of a class. Take advantage of this option if it's available to you because it can give you both insight into the profession and possible connections if you choose a career in baking.

One last option—try your hand at baking while at home. Invest a few dollars in a recipe book, or download some recipes from the Web sites listed in the For More Information section of this chapter, and do your own apprenticeship in your own kitchen. Bakeries may be more likely to hire you if you can demonstrate some concrete skills.

Salary

The highest-paid retail bakers belong to unions. Unfortunately, not every business that employs bakers is unionized. Union bakers can make up to $14 or $15 an hour, which is slightly higher than the wage for nonunion bakery employees. In 2000, the average baker earned an annual wage of $20,000. A baker at the top of his or her craft can make over $40,000 a year. Apprentices can expect to make less than $7 an hour when they begin their careers.

The highest-paid bakers of all are the specialists. Cake decorators who create individual and artistic designs for each item they work on can be very well paid. Bakers in this category are referred to as artisans. Pastry chefs (see chapter 4) also fall into this category.

Outlook

According to the Department of Labor, job opportunities for bakers should increase for the next few years, thanks in part to the increase in large wholesale bakers who make homemade-style baked goods for sale in stores and supermarkets. There has also been a rise in small specialty shops that offer bagels, muffins, and other baked goods to the public.

FOR MORE INFORMATION

ORGANIZATIONS

American Bakers Association

1350 I Street NW, Suite 1290
Washington, DC 20005-3300
(202) 789-0300
Web site: http://www.americanbakers.org
The voice of and advocate for the baking industry in the United States.

The Bread Bakers Guild of America

3203 Maryland Avenue
North Versailles, PA 15137
(412) 322-8275
This organization offers many resources to the professional baker, including job openings, trade articles, discussions, and much more.

WEB SITES

Baking Network

http://www.bakingnetwork.com
The Baking Network is a great resource for professional bakers. It features classifieds, employment openings, discussion groups, and a marketplace.

Nestlé's Very Best Baking

http://www.verybestbaking.com
Nestlé is a worldwide baking company, and its Web site offers recipes straight from its kitchen as well as online chats about the art of baking.

The PastryWiz Food Resource Center
http://www.pastrywiz.com
This site has all kinds of tips about decorating cakes and cookies, as well as classifieds, merchandise, and recipes.

BOOKS

Friberg, Bo. *The Professional Pastry Chef*. New York: John Wiley and Sons, 1999.
A long (over 1,100 pages) book that is considered by many to be the "pastry chef's bible," *The Professional Pastry Chef* provides the simplest recipes available for the most complicated dessert treats.

Gisslen, Wayne. *Professional Baking*. New York: John Wiley and Sons, 2000.
A comprehensive guide to baking, from flour to pastry. Contains over 600 recipes, and devotes an entire chapter to pastries.

Jaine, Tom, and Jaqui Hurst, photographer. *Baking Bread at Home: Traditional Recipes from Around the World*. New York: Rizzoli, 1996.
An easy-to-understand book full of recipes for dozens of different types of bread and bread-related recipes from around the globe.

Rodgers, Rick, ed. *The Baker's Dozen Cookbook: Become a Better Baker with 125 Foolproof Recipes and Tried-and-True Techniques*. New York: William Morrow & Co., 2001.
A great guide to successful baking, complete with solid advice on how to avoid the most common pitfalls that can ruin baked goods as they are being prepared.

PERIODICALS

American Cake Decorating Magazine
P.O. Box 14268
St. Paul, MN 55114-1629
Web site: http://www.cakemag.com
A print magazine devoted to the art and science of cake decorating.

Bakers Journal
25 Townline
P.O. Box 190
Tillsonburg, ON N4G 2R5
Canada
A print magazine that serves as the "Voice of the Canadian Baking Industry."

Chef Magazine
20 North Wacker Drive, Suite 1865
Chicago, IL 60606
A print magazine that covers the world of cooking and baking.

Equipment Solutions
Talbott Communications
521 5th Avenue, Suite 1721
New York, NY 10175
A print magazine that tests and reviews food preparation equipment for every segment of the food service industry.

Modern Baking
Penton Media
1300 East 9th Street
Cleveland, OH 44114-1503
A print magazine focusing on current issues in the baking industry.

FOOD COOPERATIVE MANAGER

Location & Hours

Coop Community

Newsletter

Food cooperatives (or co-ops) are essentially grocery stores that have a membership-driven, team-oriented approach to selling food. Most co-ops consider themselves "buying agents," which means they exist as an alternate source of products for consumers. They are run by the members of the community, for the community.

Some of the people who shop at food co-ops are even partial owners. If you watch what you eat and want to get involved with your local community at the same time, you should explore what your local food co-op has to offer.

Job Description

The jobs at your average food co-op are very similar to the jobs a person would have at a supermarket or large food store. Most co-ops have department managers and buyers, and in some cases a manager also does the buying for his or her department, whether it is produce (vegetables), beauty aids, or baked goods. A good buyer/manager needs to know what is and what isn't in stock. Additionally, he or she also needs to know when the out-of-stock items will be available again. Department managers report to a general manager who is responsible for the day-to-day running of the co-op, which can include processing payroll and dealing with employee concerns.

Vicki Reich is the food buyer at the Moscow Food Co-op located in Moscow, Idaho. She began as a volunteer there and worked her way up to her current position, stopping along the way to perform the jobs of maintenance person, delicatessen worker, baker, cashier, and nonfood buyer over the course of two years. "My job grew as the store grew," Reich says. "I used to work alone, but

Park slope food coop

About the coop	How to Join
Location & Hours	The coop Matters
coop community	Recipes
Newsletter	General Meeting
Shift Swap	Events calendar
Links	work Schedule

MORE THAN GOOD FOOD AT GREAT PRICES

Today is Monday in Week A

A COMMUNITY IN PARK SLOPE AND BEYOND

Home	Newsletter	Hours
classifieds	work Schedule	Links

Park Slope Food Coop
782 Union Street, Brooklyn, NY 11215
United States
Telephone: 718-622-0560

as the co-op expanded, I needed the help of the two assistants I have now."

The best way to get your foot in the door is to volunteer, and most co-ops require that their members do so anyway to enjoy the benefits of their memberships. By working as a co-op volunteer, you have the opportunity to become familiar with the routine. This exposure will make obtaining a paid position easier.

The lowest paid positions at co-ops usually involve the receiving and preparation of food, such as food servers (if the co-op has a delicatessen or bakery), and stock workers, who unload the shipments that buyers order. The next level of paid workers includes cashiers, cooks, bakers, assistant managers, and buyers. Since co-ops are very democratic in the way they are run, most employees have spent their share of time working in lower-level positions before graduating to better-paying jobs.

"The general manager of our co-op started as a volunteer," Reich relates. "She worked her way up by performing well and having the desire to move up through the ranks."

Many food cooperative managers maintain Web sites to help foster the community feel of their establishments.

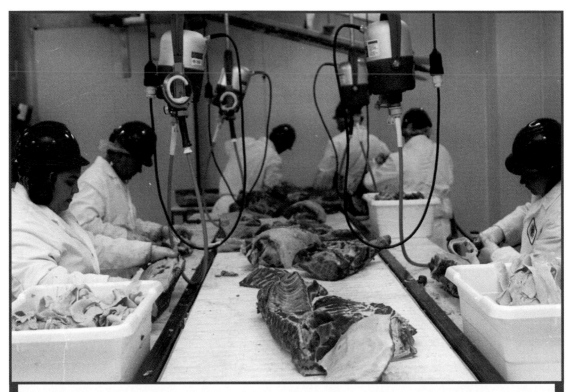

Small farmers founded this food co-op in Dawson, Minnesota, where workers are shown processing meat. The co-op was started to compete with larger meat packers that had been crowding them out of the market.

Another benefit of working at a co-op is the sense of community that helps to create a friendly and enjoyable atmosphere. Since co-ops are not run solely for profit, the employees and customers may enjoy greater control over the products they want to buy.

Many co-op employees are able to make a living wage that may be slightly less than some other food-related jobs, but the democratic principles that a co-op is based on and the fair and friendly environment are a welcome change for many people. Reich adds, "If you can handle not being a millionaire and enjoy what you do, then I call that success."

Education and Training

The best way to get started at a food co-op is to simply walk in and ask any questions you may have. Sign up as a member and see if you enjoy the environment. If the membership fee is too much for you, ask if you can work for free for the experience. Training, as with many jobs in food markets, is accomplished by hands-on work.

Salary

Pay rates for employees of a co-op vary by position, location, and membership. A larger food co-op with six or seven years invested in the business is more likely to pay a higher wage than a co-op that has been formed in the last six months. The manager of a co-op will obviously earn a higher salary than buyers or cashiers.

Outlook

Food cooperatives seem to be on the rise. There are approximately 300 food co-ops in the United States, and it would be difficult to travel to foreign countries and not find some sort of cooperative businesses in operation. Over 100 million people in the United States are members of some type of co-op. They may not all deal in fresh produce and groceries, but the movement toward consumer-owned businesses continues to grow each year.

FOR MORE INFORMATION

ORGANIZATIONS

The International Co-op Alliance (ICA)
15, route des Morillons
1218 Grand-Saconnex
Geneva, Switzerland
+41 22 929 88 88
Web site: http://www.ica.coop/ica/index.html
The ICA is an international group that represents the interest of cooperatives worldwide.

National Cooperative Business Association
1401 New York Avenue NW, Suite 1100
Washington, DC 20005
(202) 383-5440
Web site: http://www.ncba.org
Discusses more than ten different co-op types and has a page that details the start-up and operation of a food cooperative.

WEB SITES

Food Co-ops and Other Co-op Resources
http://www.columbia.edu/~jw157/food.coop.html
A great directory put together by Columbia University in New York City that details food co-ops by state and country. There are some informative links, too.

BOOKS

Birchall, Johnston. *Co-op: The People's Business*. Manchester, England: Manchester University Press, 1994.

A general history of the co-op, with some good insight into the benefits of cooperative living and buying.

Claiborne, Craig, and Pierre Franey. *The New New York Times Cookbook*. New York: Random House, 1995.
A comprehensive cookbook used by chefs, containing over 1,000 recipes, including ethnic and regional cuisine.

Diamond, Marilyn. *The American Vegetarian Cookbook from the Fit for Life Kitchen*. New York: Warner Books, 1990.
An informative cookbook with a special focus on vegetarian cooking and nutritious recipes for at-home use.

Good, Phyllis Pellman, and Louise Stoltfuz. *The Central Market Cookbook: Favorite Recipes from the Standholders of the Nation's Oldest Farmer's Market, Central Market in Lancaster, Pennsylvania*. Intercourse, PA: Good Books, 1989.
Recipes and cooking tips from the vendors of the nation's first farmer's market. The 300 mouthwatering and healthy menu items and pictures make this a good resource.

Reuben, Richard. *The Farmer's Market Cookbook: Seasonal Recipes Made from Nature's Freshest Ingredients*. New York: Lyons Press, 2000.
A cookbook for people who want to cook with fresh products, some of which are available only in certain seasons. A great reference for greengrocers and people who buy produce from them.

Rombauer, Irma S., et al. *The New Joy of Cooking*. New York: Scribner, 1997.
One of the best-known cookbooks ever published, which began as a collection of recipes from friends and relatives. This new edition contains the original recipes plus new recipes that involve grains and soybeans for alternative diets.

Ronco, William C. *Food Co-ops: An Alternative to Shopping in Supermarkets*. Boston: Beacon Press, 1974.
A descriptive guide that discusses the nature of food cooperatives and how they benefit the community.

Wickstrom, Lois. *The Food Conspiracy Cookbook: How to Start a Neighborhood Buying Club and Eat Cheaply*. San Francisco: 101 Productions, 1974.
Discusses the work and investment involved in starting a small cooperative for food purchases in order to save money.

PERIODICALS

Vegetarian Times
International Subscriptions Inc.
1 Meadowlands Plaza, 9th Floor
East Rutherford, NJ 07073
Web site: http://www.vegetariantimes.com
A print and online magazine concerned with vegetarian cuisine. The magazine includes important items such as food substitutions for vegetarians, natural remedies, nutritional information, and a glossary for new vegetarians.

FOOD STYLIST

Food stylists arrange food to be professionally photographed for magazines, books, advertisements, and movies. Food stylists help create the images that bring people into kitchens, restaurants, and supermarkets.

Job Description

Food stylists are first and foremost cooks who are responsible for all of

A food stylist lays out entrées and side dishes on a table in preparation for a photo shoot. Many restaurants commission photo shoots of their fare for use in promotional materials such as brochures and advertisements.

the food items involved in a food photography shoot. Based on a client's request, they obtain ingredients, cook them, and ensure that the prepared food stays ready to be photographed, maintaining a uniform look throughout a busy day of shooting. Some shoots can last over twelve hours.

Preparing food for photographing requires many different skills. Food styling is both an art and a science. Food stylists need to truly understand the properties of the foods they cook for photo shoots in order to know how far in advance they need to be made. This includes knowing what

color an item would have if it were freshly baked or how long a food that needs refrigeration can survive outside of a cold environment.

The conditions on photo sets can be tough on food. Imagine what a pint of ice cream would look like after five hours on the set under hundreds of watts from bright lights! In cases like these, food stylists may have to chemically alter the food they've prepared or even concoct prop, or fake, food. A slight knowledge of chemistry can help—a few grains of salt or a drop or two of an inedible liquid may give the appearance of food some extra stamina. Clients usually want food to look like it has just been prepared to project appealing images to consumers, so no stylist travels too far without a kit packed with ingredients and tools to handle any situation.

Stylists must be able to work as members of a team. They work with photographers, art directors, and the client who is paying for the photos or filmed food. Some stylists may have assistants to help clean the cooking items or carry equipment.

Education and Training

Backgrounds in cooking (see chapter 4) and baking (see chapter 6) are very important for anyone who would like to try their hand at styling food. This experience can come from different

sources. Some food stylists have spent time as chefs or cooks in restaurants; some have worked in the past as personal chefs or attended culinary schools. Most culinary or cooking schools offer only coursework in food styling rather than full degrees. This is a great advantage for anyone interested in this field who may not be going to college.

As with the majority of the job opportunities in this book, despite your food background, another key step on the food stylist staircase is apprenticing. Many hopeful stylists seek employment under the instruction of an experienced food stylist. Cooking is important to styling, but the most important aspect of this profession is not taste, but presentation. A good way to become proficient in food styling may be to watch someone perform in his or her actual work environment. Working for a seasoned stylist will give you practical experience and will help you develop a portfolio, which you'll need to shop your work around when you strike out on your own. Learning all of the ins and outs of the profession can be time consuming, so be patient.

Check out some of the listings at the end of this chapter. They provide some good points of contact to help you get started.

Food stylists employ many crafty tricks that go beyond setting an attractive layout to get great food photographs. They must make sure that the chef's creation withstands the rigors of a photo shoot.

A Stylist's Toolbox

A food stylist needs to be ready for any situation that may arise during a photo shoot. Many stylists carry an ordinary fishing tackle box filled with items that are slightly different from what your average fisherman might need. Here are some items a food stylist should always have at hand.

Non-Food Supplies

Tweezers, toothpicks, cotton swabs, razor blades, oil, paint brushes, electric mixer, small blowtorch, spray bottle, hotplate, ice chest or cooler, cutting board, knives, sponges, ice-cream scoop, measuring spoons and cups, glue, plastic ice cubes, paint stripper

Food Supplies

Pepper, instant potatoes, butter, jam, olive oil, flour, rice, maple syrup, parsley, salt, cinnamon, oregano

Salary

According to Delores Custer, an internationally known food stylist, wages for food stylists increase with population. This means there is more work to be found in larger cities. One reason for this is that many magazine publishers and television companies are based in more densely populated areas.

A seasoned food stylist working in New York City can make anywhere from $350 to $850 a day. This rate may be lower in smaller cities or areas of the United States with fewer people. Stylist assistant salaries will be much lower than this and will vary for a particular employer.

Outlook

The outlook for food stylists varies. Food styling for print publications seems to be more plentiful and steadier than opportunities in television advertising and movies. More and more culinary schools are adding or planning to add food styling to the courses they offer. Perhaps one day it will be possible to obtain a degree in this interesting field.

FOR MORE INFORMATION

WEB SITES
The Art of Styling Food
http://www.ameritech.net/users/dlafferty/1FoodStylist.html
Donna Lafferty has been styling food for twenty-one years, and her business's Web site is an informative resource for clients.

Culinary Institute of America
http://www.ciachef.edu
The CIA offers thirty-hour courses in food styling for about the cost of one college credit.

Foodesigns.com
http://www.foodesigns.com
An Internet resource dedicated to food stylists everywhere. The site also offers subscriptions to the *Tweezer Times*, a magazine that it publishes. The "Style Share" link leads to a message board with questions posed and answered by real food stylists.

Foodstyler
http://www.foodstylist.com
This is Karen Templing Food Styling. Her clients have included Kraft, Pepperidge Farms, Jif, Goya Foods, and Moet & Chandon.

Food Styling
http://food4film.com
Food stylist Jacqueline Buckner works internationally to teach food styling to small groups of people. She has worked in commericals and film.

BOOKS

McGee, Harold. *On Food and Cooking: The Science and Lore of the Kitchen.* New York: Scribner, 1997.
A book that explores the science behind how food is prepared and cooked, and answers questions about cooking processes that many people normally take for granted. A good reference for food stylists who need to know how food will stay looking good on the set.

ARTICLES

"Food Styilng for Television and Film," by Phillip W. Erhardt
This article offers some good information concerning food styling for the moving image.

PERIODICALS

Bon Appétit

Condé Nast Publications
4 Times Square
New York, NY 10036
Web site: http://eat.epicurious.com/bonappetit
Print and online magazine dedicated to good food and its enjoyment. Includes articles on food, wine, and cooks' tools. The online portion, Epicurious, features the "world's greatest recipe collection."

Chef Magazine

20 North Wacker Drive, Suite 1865
Chicago, IL 60606
A print magazine that covers the world of cooking and baking.

Cook's Illustrated

Boston Common Press
17 Station Street
Brookline, MA 02445
Web site: http://www.cooksillustrated.com
A print and online magazine for the at-home cook. A great tool for chefs who strive for a personal touch.

Food & Wine

American Express Publishing
1120 Avenue of the Americas
New York, NY 10036
Web site: http://foodandwine.com
Print and online magazine containing recipes, contests, recipe slide shows, and methods of preparing health-conscious food.

Martha Stewart Living

Web site: http://www.marthastewart.com
A print and online magazine dealing with many aspects of home decoration, catering, and entertaining with food. Includes beautiful food photography and food styling tips.

Waitrose Food Illustrated
Web site: http://www.wfi-online.com
A British print and online magazine that is known as a trendsetting publication in the field of food styling.

CATERER

Catering is closely connected to the work performed by personal chefs, but the number of people that caterers cook for is usually much larger. Good caterers take principles from the professions of restaurant chefs, bakers, and food stylists, and use them to host events for large groups that are both pleasing to the eye and memorable.

Job Description

Caterers are professional hosts. They oversee many of the preparations for special events such as banquets, weddings, bar mitzvahs, and graduation parties. People often seek out catering services when they need food prepared for a large group. "Large" is relative here. It can mean anything from 5 to 5,000 people.

There are many different levels of catering. Some people may choose to cater in their spare time and run small businesses from their homes. There are also large catering companies (hotels, for instance) that may have separate catering teams who are dispatched to multiple events that are scheduled for the same day.

The food that caterers serve can vary. Some clients may request only the cheese, bread, and rolls to make sandwiches for hungry executives at a board meeting, and some may want to serve a five-course French meal. Many caterers have professional cooking backgrounds that help them immensely as caterers, whether they have worked as chefs or short-order cooks.

Many large catering companies offer catering services that include venue, waitstaff, food, and, sometimes, entertainment.

Caterers are hired for their expertise. Clients may have an idea of the food they would like at their event but value the creative menu and display suggestions of a caterer. People skills are a great help to any caterer. If a client and caterer cannot communicate, it may hurt the overall success of an event. Caterers also need to adapt quickly. For instance, if a caterer's usual supplier of vegetables is closed or out of certain ingredients, he or she cannot tell a client that the menu has to be changed. People hire caterers because they expect important functions to go smoothly and professionally. Food styling can come into play in the presentation of food at a catered event. Some themed functions may require advance setup in the form of party favors, floral displays for tables, or wall hangings.

No matter what the size of the catering company or the event, caterers must be extremely organized. Less than half of a caterer's work time is actually devoted to cooking. The rest is spent transporting food and hiring personnel. Some caterers do not own the majority of the equipment they use, and renting dishes and portable cookware is also time consuming. If they are serving alcohol at a function, they may need to visit city hall to obtain a special license.

Catering can open doors to other interesting lines of work. Some caterers move on to private party planning, which can involve hiring caterers and entertainment, or they may jump to other fields such as floral supply or equipment rental.

Education and Training

Many culinary schools offer catering classes, but they are not necessary to start a career as a caterer. Many people begin at home, experimenting with various types of cuisines in order to have a very wide base of meals from which their clients can choose. Since home catering businesses have very low overhead (operating costs), you can do it part-time to test out the market in your area. Another option is to work a few hours a week for a small caterer in your area to learn the business.

If you do start your own catering enterprise, be as aggressive as possible. Hit the pavement and post signs, and talk to other businesses that sell supplies for special events, such as flower shops and liquor stores, to see how difficult it is to obtain clients. Promote your new company in local newspapers, hang flyers, or send e-mails to family and friends. You should also consider obtaining a voluntary catering certification from one of many organizations in order to increase your marketability.

Another way to explore the business is to seek employment at a hotel or a banquet facility. These businesses are very experienced in hosting special affairs, and the experience a hopeful caterer can obtain is invaluable. Working at establishments like these will not require the initial investment you would need to start your own business.

Training for your prospective catering career does not have to begin in such a focused manner. Any time spent

In addition to preparing food, caterers must also hire waiters and waitresses to pass hors d'oeuvres, serve dinner, or assist in the buffet line. Sometimes caterers pull double duty as servers.

working in a restaurant is extremely helpful, from waiting tables (to learn customer service) to working on the chef's line (to learn the craft of cooking).

Salary

The most financially rewarding method of catering is to be self-employed. With a very low investment ($1,000 in some cases) for food, supplies, and basic equipment, it is possible to make $50,000 in a year of steady events and clients. The investment may be much higher for a professional catering

business ($75,000), but people who run catering businesses at this level can generate a six-figure profit with hard work and planning. If you decide to work for a catering company, the pay will depend on what services you perform for a particular supervisor. The goal would be to work your way up to being an integral member of a hotel or private catering team.

Outlook

The food service industry has been predicted to be one of the fastest growing fields for the next few years. In the past ten years, specialty food businesses have become increasingly popular. If you put some thought into an interesting variation on the general field of catering, the future in this line of work can be very bright.

FOR MORE INFORMATION

WEB SITES
Belgio's Catering
http://www.belgios.com
This Chicago business offers free tools for people seeking caterers, including a catering bid worksheet to help clients get the best deal possible from a caterer.

Catering Web
http://cateringweb.com
This is a great Web site for caterers and customers. Catering Web refers potential clients to caterers who register with their service. There is also a self-catering link for visitors who may be thinking of catering their very own special events.

Direct Catering
http://www.directcatering.com
A cool search engine that enables customers to search for the precise event they would like to host.

Woodstock Moveable Feast
http://woodstockmoveablefeast.com
Another small caterer with a guide on obtaining catering services.

BOOKS

Crisafulli, John, Sean Fisher, and Teresa Villa. *Backstage Pass: Catering to Music's Biggest Stars*. Nashville, TN: Cumberland House, 1998.
An interesting book filled not only with great catering recipes for large groups but also very revealing and funny stories about some of the clients served over the years by the authors, including Tina Turner, Pearl Jam, and Van Halen.

Kessler, Judy. *An Affair to Remember: Recipes, Menus, and Home-Entertaining Tips from Hollywood's Leading Caterers*. Los Angeles: General Publishing Group, 1999.
A nice collection of advice from caterers who provide services to some of the world's wealthiest and most demanding clients.

Lawrence, Elizabeth. *The Complete Caterer: A Practical Guide to the Craft and Business of Catering*. New York: Doubleday, 1992.
The name says it all.

Roman, Michael. *Catering: The Art, Science, and Mystery*. Chicago: Catersource, Incorporated, 2001.
Mr. Roman is considered the guru of catering and is an in-demand instructor and consultant. His book includes how-to's on starting and running a catering business, as well as other insightful information.

Shiring, Stephen B. *Introduction to Catering.* New York: Delmar Learning, 2000.
A good reference with interviews and a discussion of the difference between an amateur caterer and a true professional. Also includes stories describing the ups, downs, and potential mishaps that are bound to occur in the career of a caterer.

Stefanelli, John M., and Patti Shock. *On-Premise Catering: Hotels, Convention and Conference Centers, and Clubs*. New York: John Wiley and Sons, 2000.
A guide to catering large-scale events in locations that have spaces to accommodate large groups of people.

10

GREENGROCER

Do you have a green thumb? Does fresh air appeal to you? If so, and you also like to meet people, you should take a look at the job of greengrocer. Greengrocers provide a valuable service in larger towns and cities: They get the freshest fruit and vegetables to people who may not be able to get them by any other means.

Job Description

Greengrocers are basically farmers. This does not mean that you have to move to the country to become one. There are plenty of small farm owners who live within a few hours of large cities and travel to and from their farms, loaded with fresh produce. Farmers grow a variety of crops, or sometimes one or two specific ones, and take them to cities to sell.

A large number of cities in the United States have started farmers' markets in the last thirty years. For a fee, growers can rent space and sell their produce to anyone. This provides a great source of income for greengrocers and fresh produce for customers. Most open-air markets allow only regional growers to rent space. Large businesses or corporate farms are prohibited from making any sales at these markets. The greengrocers keep 100 percent of the profits from their sales.

Most open-air markets have strict rules regarding the produce that is sold. The majority of it has to be grown by the person selling. Most markets have a staff to make sure that everyone plays by the rules. This means the produce found at farmers' markets is generally fresher than that found at most supermarkets, which may come from as far away as Holland and loses flavor the longer it is off of the vine or out of the ground.

Farmers' markets also contribute to the community in which they operate. Many neighborhood residents love the

Greengrocers help a customer sift through some of their farm's varieties of organically grown tomatoes. A good greengrocer can provide valuable information about the produce that he or she sells.

chance to get fresher fruit and vegetables at prices that are the same as, if not lower than, those at larger stores. Markets are set up in designated spots in cities, such as parks and play-grounds. The largest farmer's market in the United States can be found in Union Square, in New York City, which is the heart of the downtown area. Locations like these make it easy for everyone to have access to great fresh produce. In addition, the large numbers of people shopping often result in a rise in traffic for other local businesses that don't sell produce. Being a greengrocer is also a great opportunity to develop good personal relationships with customers. Many city dwellers look forward to speaking with fruit and vegetable experts, and may ask advice on how to use certain spices or food preparation methods. Chefs who work in city restaurants love open-air markets. The ability to obtain the freshest and best-tasting produce ensures that chefs who shop at these markets can cook the best-tasting food using the finest ingredients.

Education and Training

Growing fruits and vegetables can start as a hobby and possibly develop into more of a full-time venture later on. The biggest requirement for greengrocers is land. Even if a person concentrates on one crop only, he or she needs sufficient space for vegetables and fruits to grow.

Starting a farm, even a small one, is a huge undertaking and would be very difficult to do immediately after high school. One alternative to doing this, provided you can find space, would be to take the cooperative approach (see chapter 7) and start a community garden with products and profits to be shared by all members equally.

It may be a good idea to try your hand at a crop that is easier to grow and see if your produce can fetch a fair price in the marketplace. If you know of a local farm, ask the owners if you can help them with their crops, and learn as much as you can from their experience. Growing produce is a very

Greengrocers sort and pack produce before delivering them to a local farmers' market.

demanding job that requires 100-percent dedication, and no one should try to base their main income on this profession without doing some research, both in books and in the fields.

Salary

A greengrocer's income is dependent on customers and weather. If bad weather hurts a crop, the potential for earning will definitely decrease. If you live near a city, stop by any booth at an open-air market and talk to some of the sellers.

The whole concept of open-air markets is based on a personal and friendly atmosphere, so chances are you'll find someone who can give you the best advice for the particular region in which you live.

Outlook

In 1999, Americans ate 151.9 million pounds of kiwis and 249.7 million pounds of asparagus. Just think how many of the more popular fruits and vegetables were eaten that year! The concept of the open-air market is being embraced by more and more metropolitan areas every year, so if you live near a city, becoming a greengrocer can provide you with both fresh air and a means of income.

FOR MORE INFORMATION

WEB SITES
Cornell University: "Food Safety Begins on the Farm: A Grower's Guide"
http://www.hort.cornell.edu/commercialvegetables/issues/foodsafe.html
This Web site has loads of tips for safe small farming, from seed planting to driving a truck full of squash to the big city.

Greenmarket: The Council on the Environment of New York City
http://www.cenyc.org/HTMLGM/maingm.htm
Greenmarket was established in 1976 and is gaining farming members each year.

Open Air-Market Net
http://www.openair.org
This Web site is the "World Wide Guide to Farmers' Markets, Street Markets, Flea Markets and Street Vendors." There are plenty of listings for open-air markets throughout the United States and beyond, as well as some history and very good reasons to support these markets and the people who work there.

The Organic Farmer's Marketing Association
http://web.iquest.net/ofma
Information on organic certification and standards.

The Small Farm Resource
http://www.farminfo.org
This site is a benefit to anyone who owns a farm or grows small crops. There is even a link to gardens for people who choose to concentrate on one or two crops.

USDA (United States Department of Agriculture) Farmer Direct Marketing
http://www.ams.usda.gov/directmarketing
A site run by the USDA with plenty of information on financial resources for people who want to become involved with farmer direct marketing.

USDA Rural Information Center
http://www.nal.usda.gov/ric/faqs/farmfaq.htm
The RIC has very sound advice for people who may want to start a small farm. The above address will take you directly to their FAQ (Frequently Asked Questions) page.

BOOKS

Coleman, Eliot, Sherri Amsel, and Molly Cook Field. *The New Organic Grower: A Master's Manual of Tool Techniques for the Home and Market Grower*. White River Junction, VT: Chelsea Green Publishing Company, 1995.
A guide for dedicated and serious gardeners and hopeful market growers, with extensive advice on winter growing, organic vegetables, soil fertilization, and weed control.

Corum, Vance, Marcie Rosenweig, and Eric Gibson. *The New Farmer's Market: Farm Fresh Ideas for Producers, Markets, and Communities*. Auburn, CA: New World Publishing, 2001.
A good source of information to start a business as a vendor at a farmers' market for people with farms already in place, or for individuals who would like to try this line of work.

Macher, Ron, and Howard W. Kerr Jr. *Making Your Small Farm Profitable*. Pownal, VT: Storey Books, 1999.
An ecologically friendly guide to running a small farm, with an examination of twenty farmers across the United States who are making a living by working the land.

Salatin, Joel, and Allan Nation. *You Can Farm: The Entrepreneur's Guide to Start and Succeed in a Farming Enterprise*. Swoope, VA: Polyface, Inc., 1998.
A positive view of farming through alternative methods with a focus on the small farm, but also highlighting sound business methods that can apply to any small operation.

Schwenke, Karl, and Ben Watson. *Successful Small-Scale Farming: An Organic Approach*. Pownal, VT: Storey Books, 1991.
A superb guide for small-scale farmers containing tips on every stage of the farming process, from the purchase of land to the selling of crops.

11

FRANCHISE OWNER

Starting a business is a difficult venture, especially in the food industry. Want a little help along the way? Maybe you should think about franchising. Franchises are restaurants and food stands that are owned individually but are part of a larger business. Think of McDonald's, Burger King, and Dunkin' Donuts, all of which are franchises.

There are many types of businesses that offer franchising opportunities. Ice-cream parlors, pizza restaurants, sandwich shops, fast-food and take-out restaurants, candy shops, and family restaurants are all examples of the variety of food franchise options that exist today.

Job Description

Many franchisors have a high degree of control over the appearance and operation of a franchise. Essentially, as a franchise owner, you are paying for the use of the chain's name, which has value because of its immediate recognition. You are also agreeing to do business the franchisor's way because it has been proven to be successful in the past. Most franchisors have the final say on the operations of your franchise, from uniforms to the location of the franchise itself. For example, if you decide to open your own Captain Burgerman, the head office may turn down your site request if it is too close to another restaurant in the chain, which would potentially cost your franchise business.

Why are franchisors so concerned about these issues? Because they receive a part of your income. Some of the money your store takes in will go back to the franchisor in the form of a royalty that is determined by how much money your business takes in per month or per year. By agreeing to run a franchise, you sign a contract saying so, and if you

Frank Carney *(right)*, the owner of several Papa Johns franchises, gives a helping hand as employees fill carry-out orders at a store in Wichita, Kansas.

break the terms of that contract, you can potentially lose your business and your franchise fee.

Once you obtain the right to open a franchise, be prepared to work hard. The chance for success is high, but it involves a serious amount of time spent making sure business goes well. To save money, some franchise owners pull double duty and act as the managers of their restaurants. The work can be hard, but since you'll be operating under the name of a well-known chain, you'll be given plenty of support. Both you and the franchisor will be concerned about the income of your franchise. If it succeeds, it will be rewarding for everyone.

Education and Training

Technically, a high school diploma is all you need to enter the franchising game. Running a franchise requires intensive research. Once you've secured an initial investment, you should explore all of the franchise options that are available. A good way to do this is to attend a franchise exposition. These are usually held in convention centers or large venues and give prospective franchise owners a chance to "window shop." Seeing many different franchisors can help you decide which business is the right one for you.

It is logical to choose a franchise that offers the maximum support for the minimum royalty payment. Many franchises have short-term schools in which they teach you the basics of running a business. Some franchises continue to offer support in the form of manuals and toll-free assistance lines to the franchise owners they work with.

Salary

The salary in this business depends on a few things, such as the location of the franchise, the competition, and the way a business is organized and run. As the owner of a franchise, your salary will come out of the net profit, which equals all

Working your way up from food server to manager in a fast-food restaurant can give you a good insight into what it takes to run your own franchise.

of the money made before taxes, payroll, and other business expenses. Many franchise owners do not pay themselves too much when their business is starting out, opting to put money back into their business. However, the average net income for a franchise can average from $200,000 to $2 million a year.

Outlook

The outlook for franchising is great. A new franchise opens up every eight minutes in the United States. According to the

International Franchise Association, franchises currently make up 40 percent of all sales by U.S. businesses. Also, there are many franchises that started in the United Stated that have satellite operations all over the world. If you like to travel, opening a franchise in another part of the world could be for you.

FOR MORE INFORMATION

WEB SITES

Abracat Franchise Center
http://www.abracat.fransol.com
A great site! Abracat explains the entire franchising process and gives advice on how to start your business, a glossary, and recommended reading to increase your franchise knowledge.

FoodFranchise.Com
http://www.franchise.com
This site is for people with slightly more of an idea of how franchising works. There is a useful feature that allows you to search for a franchise based on the minimum investment.

FranchiseMoney.com
http://www.franchisemoney.com
A funding advice and location Web site.

Small Business Administration (SBA)
http://www.sba.gov
The SBA's Web site has great information on financing and starting a franchise.

BOOKS

Arden, Lynie. *200 Franchises to Buy: The Essential Sourcebook for Evaluating the Best Franchise Opportunities.* New York: Broadway Books, 2000.
A look at the most successful franchise opportunities in terms of financing, marketing, and training.

Keup, Erwin J. *Franchise Bible: How to Buy a Franchise or Franchise Your Own.* Central Point, OR: Oasis Press/PSI Research, 2000.
A comprehensive look at the entire process of obtaining funding for a franchise, as well as assistance with choosing a suitable franchisor for your business.

Purvin, Robert L., Jr. *The Franchise Fraud: How to Protect Yourself Before and After You Invest.* New York: John Wiley and Sons, 1994.
A look at the frauds and scams certain unreliable franchisors attempt to use against franchise owners during and after the start-up process of a franchise, and information on how to sidestep these traps.

Rule, Roger C. *The Franchise Redbook: Easy-to-Use Facts and Figures.* Central Point, OR: Oasis Press/PSI Research, 1999.
A handbook on running a franchise, complete with statistics and figures for business prospects in the United States and Canada.

Rule, Roger C. *No Money Down: Financing for Franchising.* Central Point, OR: Oasis Press/PSI Research, 1998.
A resource on obtaining seed money to enter the fast-paced world of franchise ownership.

Seid, Michael, and Dave Thomas. *Franchising for Dummies.* Foster City, CA: IDG Books Worldwide, 2000.
The very popular "Dummies" series of books offers a plain and simple handbook on virtually all of the ins and outs of the franchising business, from simple planning to more complex issues.

Shivell, Kirk, and Kent Banning. *The Franchise Kit: A Nuts-and-Bolts Guide to Owning and Running a Franchise Business*. New York: McGraw-Hill, 1995.
Over twenty-five years of interviews and experience in the world of franchising help make this an informative guide to the world of franchising.

Thompson, Nicole, and Robert E. Bond. *Bond's Franchise Guide 2001.* Oakland, CA: Source Book Publications, 2001.
This handy reference offers 2,300 varieties of franchise opportunities in over fifty categories and a helpful list of additional contact numbers for hopeful franchisees.

Tomzack, Mary. *Tips and Traps when Buying a Franchise*. New York: McGraw-Hill, 1994.
The ABC's of franchising, with great advice on the hiring of competent and reliable employees to make your franchise as successful as possible.

PERIODICALS

Franchise Times
2500 Cleveland Avenue North, Suite G South
Roseville, MN 55113-2728
"The news and information source for franchising" is a print magazine that includes good information on the latest breaking news in the field.

12

ICE-CREAM MAKER

Almost everybody loves ice cream. Have you ever thought of using it to launch a career? Read on for information about starting your own ice-cream business. Just remember not to eat all of your merchandise!

Job Description

Making your own ice cream used to be a very difficult and labor-intensive process. Today, thanks to technology, it is easier and cheaper to produce quality ice cream in your kitchen. The earliest machine manufactured for home use is the manual ice-cream churn. A churn is basically a bucket with a motor on top that is run by old-fashioned elbow grease—hand cranking. This machine is not for weaklings. Making a batch of ice cream with one of these machines requires over a half-hour of constant turning. The benefit of hand cranking your ice cream is that you have total control over the entire process, which means you can experiment with texture and taste more freely.

The majority of home ice-cream makers these days run on electricity rather than human energy. There are more expensive machines that have their own freezers built in and literally require the push of one button to make a quantity of ice cream.

Some kitchen experience helps the process along because there are ingredients that need to be measured and mixed. Milk and ice alone don't make ice cream—you'll also need sugar, eggs (for some recipes), and whatever flavorings you decide to use for your batch. These make up what is called custard, which, when frozen, gives us ice cream.

Education and Training

The only education you need for this job is the instruction manual to an ice-cream churn and a few different recipes.

Invent your own. Who knows? Maybe the world is finally ready for Zucchini Maple Swirl! Once you've practiced making ice cream, ask your family and friends to sample your creations. Listen carefully and take their advice on how to improve your recipes. Taste buds don't lie—major food manufacturers pay millions of dollars a year to food testers, so value the free advice.

Once you become a skilled ice-cream maker, the next step will be to organize. This includes finding out where to get the best-tasting yet cheapest ingredients to make your product as original as possible. Try not to be so economically minded that it hurts the quality of your product.

When you feel you have it all down to a science, you should try to sell your wares. Explore the cost of packaging and health safety issues for the manufacturing of food before you take your product to the streets. There are plenty of small businesses that like to carry homemade foods and desserts to give their businesses a unique touch. Try local gourmet shops and caterers. Many communities have arts-and-crafts fairs—set up a stand and show them your art. Sell it to your family's coworkers or relatives. If you are serious

Making ice cream is fairly easy and can be accomplished in your kitchen. Ice-cream makers need to make sure the taste is consistent, so keeping track of ingredients and measurements is important.

Inventors William Schroeder *(right)* and T. J. Paskach check ice cream from their Nitro ice-cream maker, a machine that freezes ice cream faster than any other method.

about starting a business and hit the ground running, you will see results.

Obviously, this is a venture that should be attempted in your spare time to see if it will be a financially successful project. Many small food businesses start at home; you can do it, too.

Salary

The salary you can earn making ice cream ranges from very little money to large sums, but you should be realistic.

The History of Ice Cream

It seems the Chinese were among the first cultures to experiment with frozen desserts. They mixed snow with sweet syrups, and this knowledge was taken to Venice, Italy, by visiting Arab traders. More primitive forms of ice cream have been floating around for hundreds of years. Emperors of the Roman Empire would have their servants travel into the mountains to get fresh mountain snow to mix with fresh fruit and other sweet ingredients.

One of the first recorded appearances of ice cream was in 1782 in Philadelphia; at the time it was called "iced cream." Ice cream as we know it (using a salt/ice mixture to make a smooth, creamy dessert) was perfected in Italy in the late 1500s. Ice cream was originally a luxury for very wealthy and important people. Legend has it that one summer, George Washington spent $200 (about $2,200 today) on ice cream alone.

The French had their turn in ice-cream development as well and are noted as the inventors of the ice-cream machine. Since then, many variations on the formula have been tried, as well as the addition of many toppings. The ice-cream soda, banana split, and Chipwich are all part of a long and sweet history.

Ice-cream income is going to depend on simple math: what you sell the ice cream for minus what you spend out of your pocket to make it. That amount is your profit. Some of this money needs to go back into your business, no matter what stage it's in. You can use it for research and development of new flavors, or use it to buy better equipment that makes more ice cream faster.

Outlook

The average American eats approximately twenty-three quarts of ice cream each year, and 98 percent of all households purchase it. That's a huge market. To make money in this line of work, you don't need to supply every American with their annual twenty-three quarts—one or two spread out over many customers in your city or community could be enough to make a living.

FOR MORE INFORMATION

ORGANIZATIONS

National Ice Cream and Yogurt Retailers Association (NICYRA)
1841 Hicks Road, Suite C
Rolling Meadows, IL 60008
(847) 934-0926
Web site: http://www.nicyra.org
This organization has members in Canada, the United States, and all over the world. It exists as a good resource to exchange information with other ice-cream retailers (big and small) to make businesses as profitable as possible.

WEB SITES

Ben & Jerry's
http://www.benjerry.com
These two guys did it! With $12,000 (a good part of which was borrowed), they started their own ice-cream business, ran a very successful company, and sold it to a corporation for a large sum of money.

The Ice Cream Parlour
http://www.dsuper.net/~zaz/icecream
A site with dozens of interesting recipes for ice cream.

The Pastry Wiz
http://www.pastrywiz.com/archive/category/icecream.htm
This Web page has some out-of-the ordinary ice-cream and ice cream–based recipes from the perspective of a professional chef.

Perfect Kitchen by Essetti
http://www.essetti.com
Follow the link to "Gelato Recipes" for an explanation of the different types of frozen treats (ice cream, sorbet, gelato) and an outstanding recipe for each variety. There's even a recipe for avocado ice cream!

BOOKS

Burgoyne, John, and Christopher Kimball. *How to Make Ice Cream: An Illustrated Step-by-Step Guide to Perfect Ice Cream, Gelato and Sauces.* Boston: Boston Common Press, 1997.

Cohen, Ben, and Jerry Greenfield. *Ben & Jerry's Double Dip: Lead with Your Values and Make Money, Too*. New York: Simon & Schuster, 1997. The world-famous ice-cream makers share their views on the combination of sound business and sound social values to return something to individual communities.

Damerow, Gail, and Patricia Hobbs. *Ice Cream! The Whole Scoop.* Lakewood, CO: Glenbridge Publishing Limited, 1995.
A comprehensive guide for ice-cream makers. This handy volume also includes recipes using soy milk, rice milk, and other alternatives for people with dietary concerns.

Johns, Pamela Sheldon, and Joyce Oudkerk-Pool. *Gelato! Italian Ice Cream, Sorbetti & Granite.* Berkeley: Ten Speed Press, 2000.
A volume of recipes and information for more advanced and experienced ice-cream makers.

Lager, Fred "Chico." *Ben & Jerry's: The Inside Scoop*. New York: Crown, 1994.
This book covers the background and history of these ice-cream moguls from their first meeting in seventh grade to the early 1990s, when they began to achieve recognition.

Liddell, Caroline, and Robin Weir. *Frozen Desserts: The Definitive Guide to Making Ice Creams, Ices, Sorbets, Gelati, and Other Frozen Delights.* New York: St. Martin's Press, 1996.
Another advanced volume of innovative recipes for ice cream that rely heavily on the cooking and measuring abilities of the reader.

Simmons, Colleen, and Bob Simmons. *From Your Ice Cream Maker: Ice Creams, Frozen Yogurts, Sorbets, Sherbets, Shakes, Sodas.* San Leandro, CA: Bristol Publishing Enterprises, 1994.
This book contains over 100 recipes to try at home with a hand-cranked or electric ice-cream maker. Perfect for starting a business.

13

FOOD CRITIC

Have you ever read a restaurant review? Did you then go to the restaurant and disagree with what the critic had written? Have you ever thought that you could write a better review? If so, becoming a food critic may be an avenue for you to explore.

What are the perks? You usually don't have to pay for the meals you review, and each new restaurant is a brand-new dining experience, even if you don't particularly care for the food. Food critics have great jobs because they get to share their love of food and the enjoyment of eating it with viewers and readers.

Job Description

The first requirement is writing ability. People don't want to read reviews that describe a meal as "good" or "OK." Food critics are expected to give readers expert advice on food and a sense of the entire experience of a particular restaurant. This includes a restaurant's décor (the way it looks), service, and overall vibe. Even the way food is presented on the plate when it is delivered to a table is something readers should be told. Good food critics observe as much as they can in order to make readers feel like they were seated at the table with the reviewer. If the food is great, but the waiter accidentally drops a stick of butter down a reviewer's back, the review may not be too favorable.

A large vocabulary is also a plus for food critics. "The rosemary trout was purely atrocious," adds more spice to a review than simply writing, "I did not care for the fish." Another necessity for aspiring food critics is a solid knowledge of food and the way it is prepared. Some critics have worked in kitchens as cooks or chefs. Culinary school is not required, but a few short courses here and there may help.

Food critics Tim and Nina Zagat, who publish restaurant reviews in the *Zagat Survey*, sample a dessert at a New York restaurant.

Knowing how food is prepared gives food critics a better idea of how a meal should taste and provides the ability to identify good and bad aspects of certain dishes.

Scaredy-cats need not attempt this profession. If you took a solemn oath never to eat a snail as long as you live, you may be in for a short-lived career as a food critic. Good critics must be able to eat adventurously and often. Some food critics may need to make multiple trips to the same eatery if its menu is varied.

Local news shows, radio programs, newspapers, and magazines are the usual employers for food critics. Many critics review food for a number of publications or have an additional job. The average critic with steady employment reviews one or two restaurants per week, which may not provide enough money on which to live. Television jobs pay much more, but they are usually reserved for very experienced critics.

Another piece of advice: Be honest and fair. The word "critic" doesn't always have to be negative. If the food is not very good, a wise critic might make recommendations or give suggestions on how to improve a certain meal or restaurant.

Education and Training

The great news is that there are no degrees given in the area of food criticism. To enter this line of work, continually work on your writing and knowledge of food. You may think about joining the school newspaper and review restaurants for it. Also, consider interning (working for free to gain experience) part-time at a local newspaper or television show that reviews food regularly. Try a few sample reviews on your own, and see what the local newspaper's or magazine's editor thinks. This is a good way to get solid and honest feedback on your writing. Food critics usually write for the "Weekend" or "Lifestyles" sections of newspapers. See if there is a local public-access television food show in your area—this could be another source of experience and information for the future.

If none of these avenues are open to you, take a trip to your local library and browse through cookbooks and books on food. Subscribe to a food magazine and read its reviews, or watch food shows on cable channels devoted to food. The key is to get involved in this industry early. You may want to try cooking exotic foods at home or experimenting with gutsy choices at nearby restaurants. Try as many different types of food as possible to expand your palette. Most important, these are all fun ways to learn about a prospective job.

Remember, if people like their jobs, they usually like to talk about them. Go to a television station or newspaper. Contact a food critic via e-mail and ask him or her questions about his or her job. The critic may know about employment opportunities or may be able to advise you on how to get started.

Salary

Food critics' salaries differ, depending on the publisher of their reviews. A critic whose work is placed in a monthly national magazine may be able to make more money than someone who writes for the county newspaper. Food critics are writers and can be paid per word or per article.

This is determined by an individual publication. Contact various magazines or papers to see what each one offers food writers.

Outlook

Competition is very tough in this profession—who wouldn't want to eat great food and get paid to write about it? More food critics can be found in areas with larger populations because there are more employers who can provide employment. A small city may have only one newspaper, but large cities like Los Angeles, Toronto, or Chicago may have three or four daily publications.

FOR MORE INFORMATION

WEB SITES
Chowhound.com
http://www.chowhound.com/main.html
Chef Jim Leff runs this Web site dedicated to food lovers. Experts and nonexperts give their opinions on restaurants in different areas of the country.

CrankyMediaGuy.com

http://www.crankymediaguy.com/review.html

The Cranky Media Guy's Web site reviews fast food in a humorous way. The reviews are very funny, but they still provide good information about restaurants.

The Empty Bowl

http://www.emptybowl.com

A fun site that is dedicated to the eating and reviewing of breakfast cereals!

Food Critic James Ward

http://abclocal.go.com/wls/news/ward

James Ward is the food critic for a television station in Chicago. He has a college degree, but it is unrelated to food. Check out his work biography.

Food Critic Polly Campbell

http://www.makingitcount.com/jobscareers/careers/cc_cAMpbell.asp

Polly Campbell works for the *Cincinnati Enquirer* and offers some good advice on the duties of a food critic.

BOOKS

Bourdain, Anthony. *Kitchen Confidential: Adventures in the Culinary Underbelly*. New York: Ecco Press, 2001.

Written by a chef, this book is a hilarious and sometimes unsettling look into what goes on in the kitchens of restaurants worldwide. A good source of laughs and information for any food critic.

Chatto, James. *The Man Who Ate Toronto: Memoirs of a Food Critic*. Toronto: Macfarlane, Walter & Ross, 1998.

The adventures of a food critic who had the opportunity to dine in every restaurant (good and bad!) in Toronto, Canada.

Fisher, Mary Frances Kennedy. *The Art of Eating.* Foster City, CA: IDG Worldwide Books, 1990.
A collection of food essays that covers the science of eating and food preparation, as well as a little bit of food history and its relation to the world of today.

Hughes, Holly, ed. *Best Food Writing 2001*. New York: Marlowe & Co., 2001.
A collection of the best essays and articles written on the subject of food in 2001. The fifty-one authors discuss home cooking, international dining, and the love of food—a requirement for any food critic.

McGee, Harold. *On Food and Cooking: The Science and Lore of the Kitchen*. New York: Scribner, 1997.
A book that explores the science behind how food is prepared and cooked, and answers questions about cooking processes that many people normally take for granted.

Steingarten, Jeffrey. *The Man Who Ate Everything.* New York: Knopf, 1997.
A food editor for *Vogue* magazine, Steingarten describes his love affair with food and the distances he traveled in his career to find as much variety as he could.

White, Pamela. *Fabjob.Com. Guide to Become a Food Writer,* 2002. Available for order at http://www.fabjob.com/foodwriter.asp.
This e-book (also available on CD-ROM) walks hopeful critics through the necessary steps to get their reviews published and read by a hungry public.

CULINARY TOUR GUIDE

If you'd like to combine a love of good food, history, and possibly travel, spend some time thinking about conducting culinary tours. This is a field of employment where you can work for a travel or tour company, or maybe even for yourself! Tour guides get paid for traveling and learning about parts of North America or even the world.

Job Description

Tour guides show people the features of a city, town, or region of a country. They must be good communicators, friendly, and knowledgeable about the points of interest in a particular area. There are tour guides in every corner of the world. Conducting food tours is simply a very specialized aspect of this profession.

Food tours usually focus on either a specific type of cuisine or a certain locale. On a trip to New York City, it would be easy to find tour guides to assist you in discovering all sorts of food, since the population is so diverse. An entire weekend could be spent visiting the Greek restaurants of Queens or the Chinese eateries and markets of Chinatown, for example.

Many cities offer walking food tours of some of the ethnic areas that contribute to the diversity and appeal of largely populated areas. Some smaller towns may conduct "home-cooked" food tours for people who live in busier regions of the country. Tour guides are part of the hospitality industry, which means that customer service is a very important part of the job. This includes helping tourists feel comfortable in areas they may not be familiar with.

Tour guides can work alone or for a tourism company. Working alone makes attracting clients more challenging because of the lack of resources (such as access to

A winery guide explains the wine-making process to a tour group at the Robert Mondavi Winery in Napa Valley, California.

restaurants and funds) that companies with an operational history may have.

Tour guides may also be required to travel a great deal for their jobs. Many tour guide jobs are seasonal, and work does tend to slow down in colder weather. One solution to this is to travel with the work. Some people work as tour guides in different areas during different seasons, which involves working for more than one employer.

Education and Training

Depending on the type of service, tour guides will need some training. If you are conducting tours in another country, for example, some language skills will be beneficial to you. The best way to become a member of this industry is to work at it while you are in school. Many companies offer summer employment opportunities for high school students. Some are domestic (within North America), and some may require travel overseas. Regardless of the location, the experience will be a great help when trying to land a part- or full-time tour guide job after school. For now, learn as much about food and its history as possible, and brush up on your geography and public-speaking skills.

Salary

Wages are usually paid on an hourly basis for tour guides, starting at around $8 an hour. With experience and a record

Tourists watch cheese porters carry rounds of cheese at a Dutch cheese market. Food tour guides should try to anticipate questions about the traditions and processes associated with the food industries they show.

of hospitable guiding, it is possible to increase your wage to as high as $18 an hour. Often, members of a tour group may tip the tour guide if the tour was particularly informative or memorable. If you are in the business of being a tour director for a successful company, you could make anywhere from $200 per day and upward.

Outlook

The *Los Angeles Times* predicted in 2000 that tourism will grow faster than the general economy until 2005. As people become more knowledgeable about food, their interest will translate to vacations that revolve around eating.

FOR MORE INFORMATION

WEB SITES

Fodor's
http://www.fodors.com
Fodor's is a company that is dedicated to helping people find their way around the globe as comfortably as possible. With a guidebook covering every major city and country worldwide, Fodor's publications are well known as great sources of information for travelers and tour guides alike.

BOOKS

Berman, Eleanor, and John Coburn. *New York Neighborhoods: A Food Lover's Walking, Eating, and Shopping Guide to Ethnic Enclaves in New York's Boroughs.* Guilford, CT: Globe Pequot Press, 2001.
A 300-page guide devoted to the millions of choices that exist for dining in the five boroughs that make up New York City. An excellent resource.

Sterling, Richard, ed. *Food: A Taste of the Road* (Travelers' Tales Guides). San Francisco: Travelers' Tales, Inc., 2002.
A collection of sometimes humorous and always entertaining essays connecting food and travel to the world outside the United States and Canada.

PERIODICALS

Bon Appétit
Condé Nast Publications
4 Times Square
New York, NY 10036
Web site: http://eat.epicurious.com/bonappetit
Print and online magazine dedicated to good food and its enjoyment. Includes articles on food, wine, and cooks' tools.

Chef Magazine
20 North Wacker Drive, Suite 1865
Chicago, IL 60606
A print magazine that covers the world of cooking and baking.

Fine Cooking
The Taunton Press
63 South Main Street
P.O. Box 5506
Newtown, CT 06470-5506
Web site: http://taunton.com/finecooking
A print and online magazine for chefs and people who like to cook at home. The Web site has a special link to the Cooks Talk Forum, a newsgroup for professional chefs, amateur chefs, and everyone in between.

Food & Wine
American Express Publishing
1120 Avenue of the Americas
New York, NY 10036
Web site: http://foodandwine.com
Print and online magazine containing recipes, contests, recipe slide shows, and methods of preparing health-conscious food.

Gourmet

Condé Nast Publications
4 Times Square
New York, NY 10036
Web site: http://www.condenet.com/mags/gmet
Print and online magazine that uses travel and a love of food to examine great food across the globe.

National Geographic Traveler

National Geographic Society
1145 17th Street NW
Washington, DC 20036-4688
Web site: http://www.nationalgeographic.com/media/traveler
Print and online magazine that "aspires to live up to its tagline: 'Where the Journey Begins' and to be the source for the active, curious traveler."

Travel + Leisure

American Express Publishing
1120 Avenue of the Americas
New York, NY 10036
Web site: http://www.travelandleisure.com
Print magazine containing articles on travel, accommodations, and fine dining throughout the world.

GLOSSARY

apprentice A person who works under the supervision of a professional while he or she learns the basics of a job.

artisan A craftsman.

cash out When a food server collects his or her wages and tips at the end of a shift.

cooperative A business that is not run by a corporation, but by its own members.

culinary Relating to food.

eighty-six (86) list In restaurant language, items that are no longer being served because the kitchen has run out.

expediter Someone who works in the kitchen of a busy restaurant and helps the people who prepare the different parts of a meal make sure all the food in an order gets to a table at the same time, instead of in multiple trips.

garde-manger A chef who specializes in the preparation of cold foods, such as salads.

premial The preparation done by a food server before he or she begins serving meals.

saucier A chef whose specialty is creating sauces.

sous chef The chef who works directly under a head chef.

INDEX

About the Author

Kerry Hinton is a freelance writer and full-time food lover who lives in Hoboken, New Jersey.

Photo Credits

Cover © Jim McKnight/AP/Wide World Photos; pp. 9, 10 © Tome Campbell/Index Stock Imagery, Inc.; pp. 14, 112, 114, 134 © Owen Franken/Corbis; p. 15 © Bluestone Productions/Superstock; pp. 19, 20 © Bay Hippisley/Pictor/ImageState; p. 22 © Michael S. Yamashita/Corbis; pp. 29, 30 © Image Network/Index Stock Imagery, Inc.; p. 32 © Dan Nierling/*Waterloo Courier*/AP/Wide World Photos; p. 33 © Barrett Stinson/*Grand Island Independent*/AP/Wide World Photos; pp. 39, 40 © International Stock/ImageState; p. 42 © Mauritius/Index Stock Imagery, Inc.; p. 45 © Jaspon Platkin/*York Dispatch*/AP/Wide World Photos; pp. 49, 50 © Vecto Verso/eStock Photo; p. 52 © Tom Vano/Index Stock Imagery, Inc.; pp. 58, 59 © FotoKIA/Index Stock Imagery, Inc.; p. 61 © PhotoDisc; p. 62 © David Samuel Robbins/Corbis; pp. 68, 70 © Park Slope Food Co-op; p. 72 © Tom Cherveny/*West Central Tribune*/AP/Wide World Photos; pp. 77, 78 © Macduff Everton/Corbis; p. 80 © Victoria Arocho/AP/Wide World Photos; pp. 87, 89 © International Stock/ImageState; p. 92 © Donald Graham/Index Stock Imagery, Inc.; pp. 96, 98 © L. G. Patterson/AP/Wide World Photos; p. 100 © Ronen

Design and Layout

Evelyn Horovicz